A GIFT FOR

FROM

This coupon is good for...

This coupon is good for...

This coupon is good for...

This coupon is good for...

This coupon is good for...

This coupon is good for...

This coupon is good for...

This coupon is good for...

This coupon is good for...

This coupon is good for...

This coupon is good for...

This coupon is good for...

This coupon is good for...

This coupon is good for...

This coupon is good for...

This coupon is good for...

This coupon is good for...

This coupon is good for...

This coupon is good for...

This coupon is good for...

This coupon is good for...

This coupon is good for...

This coupon is good for...

This coupon is good for...

This coupon is good for...

This coupon is good for...

This coupon is good for...

This coupon is good for...

This coupon is good for...

This coupon is good for...